Endo

An awesome piece of work! If you're an educator who wants to transform your instructional practice and inspire the population of students you serve, then "Morning Musings" is for you.

Stacey Reed is a "highly-effective" educator, who is extremely cognizant of the powerful role educators play in the lives of their students. When you invite the Holy Spirit into your professional world, you will discover that prayer and faith go a long way to restoring joy, peace, and hope into your heart.

This book wonderfully serves educators on any level in any genre of education, as a daily reminder that persistence, diligence, discernment, and patience are all needed to do your work well—which only comes from above!

DR. LANCE R. JETER
CHIEF PRELATE
SHEKINAH FELLOWSHIP OF CHURCHES
RETIRED SUPERINTENDENT OF SCHOOLS, NEW YORK

SASHA JETER
CERTIFIED EDUCATOR, NEW YORK

I have known Stacey for some time. She has a combination of three attributes and experiences that make her perfect to author such a book. She has a strong, unwavering faith; she has an outstanding record as an educator; and she relates well to students, and their needs.

AUSTIN A. ADAMS
FORMER EXECUTIVE VICE PRESIDENT
JPMORGAN CHASE

Stacey is an experienced educator with knowledge, faith, and purpose. Her writing illustrates the best of each attribute and captures the reader's attention with ease. This text will quickly become an often read "go to" resource for educators.

TONDALEYA GREEN-JACKSON
CERTIFIED EDUCATOR
SOUTH CAROLINA

Morning Musings

MORNING MUSINGS
Weekly Encouragement for the Educator's Soul

Stacey D. Reed

ELM HILL

A Division of
HarperCollins Christian Publishing

www.elmhillbooks.com

Morning Musings
Weekly Encouragement for the Educator's Soul

Published in Nashville, Tennessee, by Elm Hill, an imprint of Thomas Nelson. Elm Hill and Thomas Nelson are registered trademarks of HarperCollins Christian Publishing, Inc.

Elm Hill titles may be purchased in bulk for educational, business, fund-raising, or sales promotional use. For information, please e-mail SpecialMarkets@ ThomasNelson.com.

Scripture quotations marked THE MESSAGE are from *The Message*. Copyright © by Eugene H. Peterson 1993, 1994, 1995, 1996, 2000, 2001, 2002. Used by permission of NavPress. All rights reserved. Represented by Tyndale House Publishers, Inc.

Scripture quotations marked KJV are from the King James Version. Public domain.

Scripture quotations marked NIV are from the Holy Bible, New International Version˚, NIV˚. Copyright © 1973, 1978, 1984, 2011 by Biblica, Inc.˚ Used by permission of Zondervan. All rights reserved worldwide. www.Zondervan.com. The "NIV" and "New International Version" are trademarks registered in the United States Patent and Trademark Office by Biblica, Inc.˚

Library of Congress Cataloging-in-Publication Data

Library of Congress Control Number: 2019906691

ISBN 978-1-400326846 (Paperback)
ISBN 978-1-400326853 (eBook)

TO MASTER JESUS.
THE WAY, THE TRUTH, AND THE LIFE.
THE ONE TRUE REDEMPTION FOR US ALL.

TO EDUCATORS WHO INSTRUCT, COUNSEL,
AND LOVE TOO—THIS ONE IS FOR YOU.

I will instruct you and teach you in the way you should go; I will counsel you with my loving eye on you.
PSALM 32:8, NIV

CONTENTS

FOREWORD

I fondly recall when I was a young boy riding to church every Sunday with my daddy and sister on my dad's bicycle. Daddy gave us four cents each; two cents for church and two cents to buy some candy. I enjoyed going to church and eating candy and sometimes imagined being the preacher or the pastor of that church. Ever since I could remember myself, I attended church weekly. However, if you lived in my parents' home, attending church was not an option.

In 1960, I became a licensed minister and in 1961, an ordained minister. I served as a pastor of four churches for 55 years. My tenure as a teacher started shortly after college graduation in 1946.

I was hired as a seventh-grade math teacher at Howard School, from where I graduated, in my hometown of Georgetown, South Carolina. I remember so well that we had large classes, but discipline was not a problem. There were no computers, so our records and data were manually completed, which was very time-consuming and resulted in many errors. We had limited resources to use in the classroom. Several teachers did not have a vehicle, so they walked to school. The salary for teachers was low. Even so, the teachers always tried to help the students achieve and remain in school, but certainly not of their own volition.

During the 1940s, prayer was allowed in schools. Most of the teachers, back then, called on God for guidance and compassion. We started the day with a prayer and reading of the scripture. Sometimes, we had a closing prayer at the end of the day. Meditating and praying became a natural habit. Teachers would often tell their success stories about God's blessings. These conversations of success were encouraging and inspiring to the new teachers and especially to me.

Stacey reminds educators that, although prayer has been taken out of some schools, prayer does not have to be extracted from their lives. They too can experience the success of God's blessings in their classroom even today.

There are many more amenities (technology, diverse teaching and learning materials, service-learning opportunities, smaller class sizes) available for today's classroom. Yet, educators still have numerous challenges today including discipline, mass school killings, and lack of parental involvement, that are overwhelming resulting in stress, teacher burnout, and a mass exodus from the teaching profession.

Therefore, educators should always pray for themselves. Meditating and praying can change educators' perspective. Executing both give educators the eyes and mindset of Christ and the heart they need to work with students.

Humble yourselves in the sight of the Lord, and he shall lift you up.

Js. 4:10, KJV

Educators, perfect attendance, extracurricular activities, GPA, well written lesson plans and technology in your classroom do not protect you from the hand of the enemy, but "prayer" does. All educators, but especially first year educators, need the strength, wisdom, protection, and understanding that comes only from God. When educators get connected, they become more humble, flexible, patient, and open to the Spirit of God. This I have witnessed.

"So, educators, cheer up, dry your tears, look up, and let God use you."

Stacey has been an educator in higher education for more than a decade. For each week's musing in this book, she shares revelatory teaching and application from her time in meditative prayer. Gleaned from her teaching and spiritual experiences, each week's musing helps educators teach with the purest of heart, mind, and intention. Meditating on them allows teachers to get in the right frame of mind to communicate with our Lord before their teaching day begins.

In her book, Stacey provides strategies for encouragement, based on the Holy Bible, that can be applied to your everyday experiences as an educator.

For I know the thoughts that I think toward you, saith the LORD, thoughts of peace, and not of evil, to give you an expected end.

JER. 29:11, KJV

Rev. Samuel A. Green, M. Div.
Retired Pastor and Educator
Former Moderator and Publishing Board Member, National Baptist Convention of America, Inc. (NBCA)

PREFACE

As an educator in today's classroom, educators cannot afford to have a morning routine that excludes meditative prayer. We should not begin our teaching day without meditative prayer. Meditative prayer has a holistic purpose, which means it is not merely for our benefit. Prayer benefits the nation, families, children, elite, middle-class, old and young, friends, colleagues, enemies, and students. Engaging in meditative prayer each morning before your teaching day transforms your soul, equipping you, through the power of the Holy Spirit, to transform your students' lives.

After earning Bachelor and Master of Arts degrees in English, I began teaching in 2007. Over the course of my teaching career, I had the opportunity to work with a wide-range of students in a variety of educational settings. Quite frankly, I am certain I would not have been able to teach effectively without the daily practice of meditative prayer cleansing my soul.

The soul is the hidden or spiritual side of the person [including] an individual's thoughts and feelings, along with heart or will, with its intents and choices.[1] To cleanse our soul, the hidden or spiritual side of ourselves, we need a relationship with God established partly through prayer.

---

[1] Willard, D. (1988). Human body and spiritual growth. Wilhoit, J. (Ed). Christian educator's handbook on spiritual formation. (especially chapters 1-7) New York: Harper and Row.
Retrieved from http://www.dwillard.org/articles/artview.asp?artID=34

Each year I taught, I was introduced to a different set of students—all with different learning styles, attitudes, and behaviors. Some days, students' resistance met my efforts to instruct. On other days, unequipped to resolve the issues in their personal and/or professional lives, resulted in misdirected anger, sass, and ultimately, failure of the course.

Sometimes, I encountered students who believed school and classroom policies did not apply to them and rebelled against those policies. In these classrooms, I also had to meet the educational needs of well-mannered students who possessed an aptitude for learning, but were caught in the crossfire of the rebellious group. All of which resulted in emotional, interpersonal, and instructional conflicts within my classroom.

And so, with each year, I amped up my teaching style and classroom management techniques. I combined learning and fun and even theoretical techniques (communication, arbitration, de-escalation) regarding classroom management, teacher-student, and student-student conflicts, but they were simply not enough to curtail the worst of behaviors and conflicts that resulted from some students as my teaching years progressed. My efforts were also not enough to provide the wisdom I needed to teach, lead, and serve both sets of students academically and spiritually. I learned only the power of God could do that.

In sharing my concerns with my spiritual mother, Mother Willa Salley, she reminded me that warfare can manifest in many forms, in anybody, and my classroom and students were no exception. She then encouraged me to pray, specifically during the morning hours, before class began and be led by the Holy Spirit.

I began to pray more and what a notable change I began to see. I found that when I prayed, the classroom experience was much more pleasant because of the work He did on my soul during each moment I spent with Him in the mornings. I realized, that no matter how impactful my lessons were, my frustrations with administration, large class sizes, average pay, and my commute to work also impacted my ability to respond with compassion and empathy, when conflicts arose. Each morning with Him illuminated a polluted area of my soul in need of cleansing, healing, and transformation.

Because I applied God's Word to my teaching day, I saw the difference in myself, teaching, student interactions, and overall classroom atmosphere. I noticed the positive differences once I began habitually incorporating meditative prayers into my morning routine. Wisdom is in His Word and when we spend time with Him, He imparts that wisdom enabling us to meet challenges we would not have otherwise thought possible.

I became more patient and attentive to my students. I became sensitive to their challenges beyond the classroom and learned to submit those challenges to God on their behalf in prayer. None of which would have been possible with a polluted soul and especially not without prayer.

Morning Musings: Weekly Encouragement for the Educator's Soul is for educators who have a desire to

- re-invigorate their soul by cultivating a relationship with Jesus Christ;
- fulfill their duties of teaching, serving, and leading with His divine wisdom; and
- transform their lives, so they can transform the lives of their students.

In this book, you get 36 musings that transformed my soul as an educator. Applying them to your life, with faith, will help you do the same.

INTRODUCTION

I am tired. I am not good enough. I simply do not measure up. I am afraid.
I am not strong enough. I don't think God hears me. I don't have enough.
I am depressed. I give up.

All are thoughts of an educator during at least one moment in their teaching career. Pair these sentiments with school violence, teacher strikes, overcrowded classrooms, and inadequate pay, and these emotions intensify. All educators can relate. We understand one another's plight. So today, I say to my fellow educators, BE ENCOURAGED! You have the fortitude to fulfill your teaching call in your season.

There were moments as an educator where I wanted to quit; give up; find a new profession, but I knew I simply could not. I was called to serve in the capacity of an educator. Each time I became content with quitting and finding a new profession, the Lord would send one of His servants to remind me of my assignment during that season. Each reminded me of the bondage God freed me from that would not have come about had it not been for the prayers of those who stewarded me. In fact, one reminded me that I needed God to successfully teach. In fact, he said, I would encounter students whom I would not be able to help with education alone, but that student would need prayer. See, the Word of God comes to deliver, instruct, and prosper us, but not only for us. It is also to bring others—yes, our students are included also—to Him and He gets the glory!

Had I given in to my desires to exit the field of teaching, I would not have been able to pray for my students and watch the power of God work miracles in their lives.

Heb. 12:4-11 teaches us who endured the most suffering of any man— past, present, and future. And yet, he still continued on to complete the mighty task of saving mankind. He did not wallow in his woes and regretted being born for such a purpose. Instead, even when his disciples fell asleep and could not pray with him for one hour, he prayed.

Educators, we have been commissioned to save our students who are the next generation of spiritual leaders, but yet are so far from God. We spend more time with them than their parents 180 days a year, so we must be in a spiritual position possessing Kingdom authority to minister, wisely, to our students. There is much opposition to the Gospel of Jesus Christ, in many forms, in our schools today; thus, we must be spiritually led in our efforts as educators to execute his will.

In doing so, we will at times, like Jesus, find ourselves alone—our colleagues and administrators asleep—while we fulfill our commission. It is in these moments, you will need power to encourage yourself and continue in the charge set before you as long as the Master has you there.

In *Morning Musings: Weekly Encouragement for the Educator's Soul,* I provide strategies for encouragement, based on the Holy Bible, that can be applied to your everyday experiences as an educator.

This book is designed to be studied alongside your Bible and offers 36 weekly musings— one for each week in the semester. Each week's musing includes **a Scriptural Reading, Weekly Teaching, Weekly Application, and Reflection.**

As you read and meditate, let each musing encourage, strengthen, and renew your soul as you prepare to teach, lead, and serve with God's wisdom.

Teacher. Servant. Leader

1. **Read the Scriptures.**
   Matt. 26:36-56, THE MESSAGE
   Matt. 23:11, THE MESSAGE
2. **Read this week's teaching on the role of the teacher as servant and leader.**

Teacher. Servant. Leader. There is only one who is a perfect embodiment of all three. He is the One great teacher, leader, and servant. Each role reflects a facet of Jesus' life. He taught, served, and led all of those who were in his care. In doing so, he provides an example for today's educators to follow in their divine assignment to teach, serve, and lead the next generation of students.

Known fondly as "Rabbi," which means "Teacher," to his disciples, Jesus was divinely aware of his responsibility to ensure accurate representation of the knowledge and wisdom he possessed. He did not allow them to puff him up, shrouding him in a cloud of arrogance. In part, his approach and demeanor are partly what made Jesus' teachings life-changing. Had Jesus allowed arrogance to overshadow his teaching, this could have potentially impacted the number of souls who stood to be saved unto our Heavenly Father simply because pride can impede impartation. Because of their inability to comprehend and receive Jesus and his works, the Pharisees ascribed pride onto Jesus' character, but they could not have been more wrong. Like so, many continued to follow Jesus being transformed by his teachings. Instead, by feeding and teaching those who looked to him for knowledge and wisdom, he served them and remained a good steward to them for our Heavenly Father entrusted them to his care.

Knowledge has the propensity to make us proud—proud of what we know and can accomplish. As an educator, this will become tempting without spiritual grounding. You will be tempted to shove your ideas upon students and colleagues as well as impose your recommendations as mandates upon them. Such temptation is a byproduct of your excitement at the chance to make a difference in your students' lives through teaching. Still, approaching your task with a servant-leader's heart, like Jesus, can surely help you to avoid this pitfall where no one benefits.

You are the purveyor of knowledge, but if you are too proud of that, your teaching approach can become condescending alienating, instead of congregating your students. The latter is what you should always aim for; you too have been given a divine assignment to teach, serve, and lead those entrusted into your care.

Certainly, if left to our own humanly limited devices, we could not teach, serve, or lead, effectively.

In fulfilling his role as a servant-leader, the one constant in Jesus' life was prayer. He always prayed to our Heavenly Father for strength, insight, guidance, and instruction to say the least. We can witness Jesus praying in the Garden of Gethsemane before his most challenging task on this earth. Instead of becoming stricken with anxiety and grief at the task before him, he prayed, and we learn in this moment, that an Angel of the Lord appeared to comfort him—Matt. 26:36-56.

You will have challenging days in the classroom ranging from behavioral challenges, to learning challenges, to teaching challenges. Each challenge can pose a hindrance to your ultimate task to teach, serve, and lead your students. But if we include the one constant of prayer in our lives, every morning, we can be confident in facing those challenges of our teaching days knowing an Angel of the Lord will also be sent to comfort us as we serve God and our students in the classroom.

Weekly Application:

As you teach, rely on your one constant (prayer) to be empowered to fulfill your role as an educator, servant, and leader in your classroom.

Reread the scriptures below.
> Matt. 26:36-56, THE MESSAGE
> Matt. 23:11, THE MESSAGE

Write the principle (s) from the scriptures you find will be most useful to you as you teach.

Reflection/Notes:

NO FEAR

1. **Read the Scriptures.**
   2 Tim. 1:7, THE MESSAGE
   2 Cor. 1:1-13, THE MESSAGE
2. **Read this week's teaching on fear.**

No Fear. Fear is an illusion the enemy manufactures to hinder progress in one or more areas of our lives and hide our purpose. Fear's purpose in the workplace is no different. Being a teacher himself, Paul was well aware of the impending failures fear could produce and was very candid about it in his letter to Timothy. You can also say that Timothy, trained by Paul, was a new educator charged with the task of sharing the Gospel of Jesus Christ. In his letter to Timothy, Paul tasks Timothy with teaching four basic essentials of the Gospel to the people: die to live with him, endure now and rule with him later, disown him, he will disown you; and remain encouraged never giving up (2 Tim. 2:11-13, THE MESSAGE).

If allowed, fear can achieve some negative accomplishments in our lives. First, fear can hinder connection. Fear disconnects educators from their students and their divine task of teaching. Many new educators, laden with fear, find it difficult to perform well in the classroom. This could be fear of students, administrators, or even parents. Either way, the fear blocks the instruction.

Fear can also suppress personalities and dictate decisions. Fear also hinders creativity. A fearful educator is unable to incorporate creativity into the instructional style or collaborate with fellow educators. Collaboration and creativity are not possible if educators are disconnected from their students and colleagues because of fear in the workplace.

Timothy associates with Paul and so becomes his understudy anointed to take his ministerial place in Lystra sharing the Gospel of Jesus Christ. (2. Tim. 10-13, THE MESSAGE). Because we identify emotionally with those closest in proximity to us, we are likely to take on some of their behaviors, actions, and emotions. Timothy certainly took on Paul's grace to teach the Gospel to an unruly bunch, which was not easy.

We know Timothy's task of teaching this content was challenging because Paul reminds him to prepare to suffer the consequences of teaching this message for Timothy's truth contrasted what Hymenaeus and Philetus believed was their truth. Timothy had a tough task ahead of him no doubt about it, but Paul reminds him of his aids to supplement his task.

1) His gift.
2) His boldness.
3) His purpose.

Timothy has a gift to teach; teaching has assigned a divine purpose to his life; and his boldness, emotionally and psychologically, prepared him to stand before a tough crowd daily. Teaching well left no space for fear to operate in Timothy's life.

When God gives us an assignment, he equips us to complete the assignment and looks over our shoulder ensuring we complete it (2 Cor. 1:1-13). We never have to fear. He does not want us to fear. As you spend time with your students in your classroom, pray against the spirit of fear and rebuke it from operating in your life and especially in your classroom.

If students sense fear from you, your task to teach life-changing content becomes jeopardized.

Fear is only successful when it is validated and not countered with 2 Tim. 1:7. We must have liberty to be who we are in Jesus Christ. As you begin to teach today, have liberty and do not validate fear in your life, but validate the love and power and sound mind God has given each one of us.

Weekly Application:

As you teach, allow God to transform your fear into courage, bold-ness, and love by verbally validating the love and power and sound mind God has given you.

Reread the scriptures below.
   2 Tim. 1:7, THE MESSAGE
   2 Cor. 1:1-13, THE MESSAGE

Write the principle (s) from the scriptures you find will be most useful to you as you teach.

Reflection/Notes:

SIMPLE TRUST

1. **Read the Scriptures.**
   Lk. 7:8, THE MESSAGE
   Jhn. 15:5, THE MESSAGE
   Acts 17:28, THE MESSAGE
2. **Read this week's teaching on simple trust.**

Simple Trust. Trust is a delicate word. To those of you who have had your trust mishandled, it is a word that has gradually disappeared from your vocabulary. But Jesus urges us to bring it back—to put it in use with the one who will never betray it. He asks us to embrace simple trust.

The Roman captain is a good example. It is his simple trust in the magnificent power of God that brings about the miraculous healing of one of his most prized servants. This Roman Captain did not deem himself worthy to make such a request of Jesus.

According to the Roman Captain, he was not a stand-up guy and neither was he proud of it. He did not reside in the biggest of mansions and quite frankly, he was embarrassed (Lk. 7. vv. 6-8). However, he did not defend his embarrassment to make him too proud to call out for Jesus' help. He admitted what he knew to be wrong within himself.

One reason many of us cannot approach Jesus with simple trust is because we believe we have to appear before him a certain way—clean, dapper, and sinless. We want to wait until we get it just right before we call out to him for help, but the facts of the Roman Captain's case prove another point.

Jesus is looking for humble, repentant, and believing men and women who will take him at his word. The Roman Captain understood the power of Jesus' words—the power in a command given by one who is in authority for he himself was a Roman Captain who rendered and executed orders (Lk. 7: vv. 6-8). So, he understood that when an order was commanded, those under the voice of the command obeyed the order—including sicknesses and ailments. When Jesus commands sicknesses and ailments to leave the body, they too must obey. The Roman captain was well aware of this and so he requests that Jesus give the order [and he knew] his servant would get well.

We learn three lessons from the Roman Captain—trust, comprehension, and belief. He trusted the authority. He understood the power of authority. And he believed in the authority. Jesus was pleasantly shocked at the Roman Captain's response for it had exhibited simple trust—trust that he had yet to come across in Israel (Lk. 7: vv. 9-10). And like so, Jesus gave the command and the servant was healed.

Jesus produces miraculous responses to our prayer requests when we genuinely exhibit simple trust in him. Today, as you humbly approach the throne of grace with your reverence and prayer requests,

1) Trust the authority (Jesus)
2) Understand the power of the authority (Jesus)
3) Believe in the authority (Jesus).
4) Make your request known to the authority (Jesus).

As educators, we are asked to place our trust in administrators, colleagues, students, financial resources, instructional resources, security and resource officers, and most often ourselves. When truthfully, apart from him, we can do nothing (Jhn. 15:5). It is in him that we live, move, and have our being (Acts 17:28). As you embark upon today's journey, I admonish you to place simple trust in Jesus Christ.

Weekly Application:

As you teach, place simple trust in Jesus Christ by openly admitting your concerns to Him and casting them upon Him, by faith, knowing He will fully protect and never leave you.

Reread the scriptures below.
Lk. 7:8, THE MESSAGE
Jhn. 15:5, THE MESSAGE
Acts 17:28, THE MESSAGE

Write the principle (s) from the scriptures you find will be most useful to you as you teach.

Reflection/Notes:

SILENT THOUGHTS

1. **Read the Scriptures.**
   Lk. 7:39, THE MESSAGE
   Phil. 4:8, THE MESSAGE
   Lk. 7: 44-46, THE MESSAGE
2. **Read this week's teaching on silent thoughts.**

Silent Thoughts. To the natural mind, what is unspoken is not heard. The Pharisee did not comprehend the spiritual significance of Jesus' presence in Jerusalem and certainly not in his home. For he extended no reverence or gratitude to Jesus from the point of his arrival to his departure. Yet, this Pharisee questioned, in his mind, the legitimacy of Jesus' spiritual authenticity. Although he did not voice it for any ears at the dinner table to hear, Jesus still heard it.

Upon witnessing the 'town harlot' enter his home and revere Jesus with her utmost honor and respect by 'raining tears on his feet, drying them with hair, and anointing his feet with the expensive bottle of perfume" (Lk. 7:36-39, THE MESSAGE), the Pharisee immediately concluded that Jesus could not be a true prophet—otherwise, he would know that this woman is a harlot and is not of good moral character. Moreso, the Pharisee could not fathom how Jesus could allow a woman with such a promiscuous past to be in his presence let alone "all over him." Yet, she was wise enough to recognize the power and presence in the room. She was not left to her own devices and thoughts; her decision to revere Jesus was not clouded by her past or the Pharisee's thoughts of her. She heard Jesus was over at his house having dinner and she made her debut.

In response to her honor, Jesus says to the Pharisee, the host of the dinner, "Do you see this woman? I came to your home; you provided no water for my feet, but she rained tears on my feet and dried them with her hair. You gave me no greeting, but from the time I arrived, she hasn't quit kissing my feet. You provided nothing for freshening up, but she has soothed my feet with perfume. Impressive, isn't it? (Lk. 7: vv.44-46). The woman's response was partly a response to what Jesus had done for her.

What will your response be to what he has already done? The school he has placed you in to teach? The students he has placed before you to teach? Will you be overpowered by your thoughts? Past? Ability? Colleagues? Boss? Lesson? Objectives? Students? Will you begin to second guess your choice to become an educator? Will you begin to doubt yourself? Or will you reverence the One who is always in the room; always able to shift an atmosphere?

As an educator, each one has the propensity to overpower you, but your thoughts are the most powerful. This is why Paul tells us in Phil. 4:8, THE MESSAGE to think on what is positive, uplifting, and reassuring. We want our audible thoughts to be filled with good cheer as well as our inaudible thoughts for Jesus hears them all. Moreso, corrupt thoughts will eventually corrupt the mind and heart resulting in wayward behavior, confusion, disrespect. Be it good, bad, manipulative, deceitful, beneficial, or generous, in spite of what we think, our thoughts do not belong to us alone. Jesus can also hear the meditations of our hearts and minds. Because of his natural perception of Jesus, the Pharisee was unable to understand Jesus' response to the woman's reverence. Importantly enough, Jesus ignores their murmurings of confusion and continues on.

In the midst of your toughest challenges in the classroom, let Jesus hear the meditations of your heart and mind for he longs to respond to those too. Treat each of your students with love, respect, and forgiveness for all of your students will not be your ideal scholar or your most well-behaved. Yet, they will still be in your classroom eager to learn and glean from what the Lord has instilled in you to disseminate to them. Above all, remember, teaching can only be successful if you shift your focus to who is always in the room.

Weekly Application:

As you teach, think positive by inviting Jesus into your day, into your classroom, and do not forget to honor and revere his presence as you talk with him. Think good, wholesome thoughts—these too can produce a miraculous response from Jesus.

Reread the scriptures below.
>   Lk. 7:39, THE MESSAGE
>   Phil. 4:8, THE MESSAGE
>   Lk. 7: 44-46, THE MESSAGE

Write the principle (s) from the scriptures you find will be most useful to you as you teach.

Reflection/Notes:

Evaluate Yourself

1. **Read the Scriptures.**
   Gal. 6:3-4, THE MESSAGE
   Pslm. 139:23-34, THE MESSAGE
2. **Read this week's teaching on evaluating yourself.**

E valuate Yourself. Many times, we accept a career opportunity without conducting a full and true assessment of ourselves. In other words, we rarely take the needed time to confirm that our values, morals, and beliefs are rooted in biblical principles before starting our careers.

Teaching is one of those careers where we cannot afford to exclude the biblical principles that should govern our lives in the classroom. It is important to know of and confess our spiritual weaknesses before we can begin to teach, serve, and lead another—especially our students.

Teaching requires discernment, wisdom, and maturity in the ways of the Spirit. Evaluating ourselves is necessary to identify our assignment, purpose, and gift and make sure each is being rightly applied to the work we have been assigned. Evaluating ourselves also helps us to identify our spiritual weaknesses. We need to pray for strength from the Almighty to fill that void each morning before we enter our classrooms.

The Bible speaks of self-evaluation at length and its importance in living, leading, and serving. Lam.3:40 tells us to search and try our ways. If any of our ways contradict those of the Lord, then we must return to Him. In Pslm. 139:23-34, the Psalmist begs the Almighty to search and help us evaluate ourselves. You must open your life privately before the Lord. He is the only One who can search your heart, inside and out, and remove all impurities setting you on the narrow path. Gal. 6:3 reminds us that those who think they are something when they are not think too highly of themselves and their efforts and abilities will surely end in failure.

Evaluating yourself helps you to identify your spiritual shortcomings and strengths, but simply knowing them is not enough. In your role to teach those students to whom you've been assigned, your spiritual strengths will be tested and the enemy will attempt to sabotage your efforts by using your weaknesses. You will not be able to rely on your natural abilities; for in your classroom, you will not be fighting a natural battle, but a spiritual one. Although you are a compendium of information in regards to your discipline, you will also need to be in regards to the knowledge of the Spirit—it is the latter that will help you to reign victorious in your spiritual battles too.

Weekly Application:

Evaluate your spiritual *-self* daily. Obey what you hear in your prayer time above all else; in prayer, the Lord will give you divine guidance. While others may not understand, you do. Allow God to use you for his glory in the life of your students.

Reread the scriptures below.
> Gal. 6:3-4, THE MESSAGE
> Pslm. 139:23-34, THE MESSAGE

Write the principle (s) from the scriptures you find will be most useful to you as you teach.

Reflection/Notes:

YOUR KNOWLEDGE.
HIS KNOWLEDGE

1. **Read the Scriptures.**
   Js. 1:5, THE MESSAGE
   1 Jhn. 2:27, THE MESSAGE
   2 Tim. 2:15. THE MESSAGE
2. **Read this week's teaching on your knowledge, His knowledge.**

Your Knowledge. His Knowledge. Knowledge is power. You've heard it. I've heard it. Although traced back to Sir Francis Bacon, countless others have said it. Generally speaking, knowledge refers to facts or data or ideas gained through experiences or education. Acquired knowledge, in any capacity, has the potential to be powerful.

While many comprehend the implications of the quote, few comprehend that the true power lies in the use of the acquired knowledge. In other words, it is the application and understanding of the knowledge that make it powerful.

In today's culture, there are many channels to information for our students. Students seek information via social media outlets, television, and news radio to name a few. Fake news has been planted in many of these outlets for the purpose of having false information disseminated. Yet, many students have adopted these outlets as a primary source of information. What's worse is sometimes, students want to use these outlets to cancel out the teacher's presence in the classroom. Nevertheless, educators are the primary agents of information in their classrooms.

As the educator, you possess a high level of knowledge in your subject-area and you equip students with that knowledge with the hopes of transforming them into a lifelong human asset to society. You teach them to understand and apply the knowledge accordingly to survive and thrive in an ever-changing society. And much like your students cannot replace your presence in their lives, you can replace the Holy Spirit's presence in your life. As you are designated to teach, guide, and advise your students, you must designate the Holy Spirit to teach, guide, and advise you. It is His knowledge that is still the most powerful. The question is how are you acquiring and using His knowledge in your life?

While you have knowledge of your subject matter to teach your students, who will you rely on to teach you the knowledge of the Spirit? The Spirit knows all things about everything and He is the ultimate teacher (1 Jhn. 2:27). His knowledge is the power we need to transform our souls, so that we can be better educators for our students. In all areas, we must study to show ourselves approved (2 Tim. 2:15) and rightly divide the Word of truth in our own lives first relying on the Spirit to teach us along the way before we can be effective in the lives of those around us. To be successful requires wisdom, which he provides generously to all who genuinely asks (Js. 1:5).

Weekly Application:

Educators, ask for His wisdom daily and in each situation where you believe you need it. Rely on the Holy Spirit's wisdom to teach, guide, and advise you, so you can teach, guide, and advise your students.

Reread the scriptures below.

    Js. 1:5, THE MESSAGE

    1 Jhn. 2:27, THE MESSAGE

    2 Tim. 2:15. THE MESSAGE

Write the principle (s) from the scriptures you find will be most useful to you as you teach.

Reflection/Notes:

VALUE IN YOU

1. **Read the Scriptures.**
    Eph. 2:10, THE MESSAGE
    Ex. 4:10-12, THE MESSAGE
    Eph. 1:4, THE MESSAGE
2. **Read this week's teaching on the value in you.**

V alue in You. On at least one occasion, most people have been on either the receiving end or giving end of favoritism. Such partial and biased treatment, in some cases, is based upon natural abilities, good looks, and popularity. Oftentimes, it has very little to do with an individual's God-given calling. In fact, people take it upon themselves to assign their value to others and choose to, or not to, qualify them based on the value they have assigned. We want our administrators, colleagues, and students to value us and our work, but we cannot desire it at the expense of true value. Educators, if you are not careful, you will allow their value to dictate your perception of your value of yourself.

Preemptively gauging the people's response to his speech impediment, Moses justifies his initial refusal to answer God's call. In Ex. 4:10-12, we also see where Moses attempts to devalue himself; yet, it is God who qualifies him and calls Aaron, his brother, to cover him. Know that people do not qualify you; God does. Value of another person is not determined by one individual or a group. We cannot even assign a value to ourselves because God has already done so before the foundations of the world. When Moses attempted to do so, he gravely underestimated his value in God's eyes. We were chosen and fashioned in Him (Eph. 1:4). Because of that, our value has already been established.

You cannot neglect your role because you disagree with your value or are unable to see the value in you that God sees. We also cannot disqualify ourselves from the calling because we devalue ourselves as an educator according to the value standard of another.

God, himself, explains that He has created all! In creating all, He has created a purpose for us all (Eph. 2:10) and we should not decide against that purpose nor come up with vain reasons for not fulfilling it. The steps of a good man are ordered by the Lord. If you're in the teaching field, there must be a purpose, be it seasonal or long-term, for your being there.

You have been chosen to not only teach a natural subject, but to verbalize His decrees in your classroom. Like Moses, it does not matter if you believe you are not qualified because you are not popular enough, tall enough, slim enough, or strong enough. When God calls you, you are enough! Moreso, when you are assigned to teach, your value has already been assigned! You have been graced to teach your students.

Weekly Application:

Confess your weaknesses and rely on God's Word to give you strength to combat thoughts of fear, inadequacy, uncertainty, and doubt you will experience as you teach.

Reread the scriptures below.
> **Eph. 2:10**, THE MESSAGE
> **Ex. 4:10-12**, THE MESSAGE
> **Eph. 1:4**, THE MESSAGE

Write the principle (s) from the scriptures you find will be most useful to you as you teach.

Reflection/Notes:

REMAIN FOCUSED

1. **Read the Scriptures.**
   Jer. 29:11, THE MESSAGE
   Gen. 50:20, THE MESSAGE
   2 Pet. 1:3-4, THE MESSAGE
2. **Read this week's teaching on remaining focused.**

Remain Focused. It is human nature to be concerned about ourselves. We believe we are responsible for our daily well-being and in some way, I suppose we are. The Lord has given us all things pertaining to Godliness and life (2 Pet. 1:3-4). This means we have the knowledge and resources that He releases unto us to care for ourselves. It is when we begin to let the concern for—*self* consume our thoughts and motivate our existence that we live out of divine order. When we no longer look to Him for what we need, our vision becomes clouded; it becomes easy to get unfocused. Lesson planning time becomes personal time. Attention to administrative duties wanes, students are seen as a nuisance, and we slowly blur the lines between personal and professional duties.

Teaching is a full-time job that can extend well beyond the work-day; it especially does for educators who opt to advise and work with students beyond the classroom to bolster learning and student retention.

Sometimes, you will feel split between your personal and professional responsibilities. Like your students, you will need structure, discipline, direction, and love. You will need to be taken care of as well. You will be busy teaching, advising, counseling, grading, to say the least, and will need care too. Your need for love, security, acceptance, approval, companionship, intimacy, and self-realization—to name a few—are all very present while you teach and do not disappear. So, do not be naïve to this fact; you are not a robot and you have these basic human needs. The longer, however, these needs are unmet, the more they become a distraction impeding your efforts to remain focused on the task at hand—teaching. What is more important, however, is to whom you submit these needs.

Because it is in these moments when your soul becomes even more vulnerable, you must submit these needs to God. Because He knows the plans He has for your life (Jer. 29:11) and He can help you create a healthy professional and personal balance. Spending time at work at the expense of your personal, familial, or spiritual well-being leads to burn-out. A just weight delights the Lord (Prov. 16:11) and alleviates you of the pressures the imbalance can yield.

The just weight also keeps you focused. In today's classrooms, educators cannot afford to be unfocused, but more vigilant than ever. He uses all of our experiences to mold us into our future selves; for an ideal role He has already ordained for our lives. (Gen. 50:20)

Weekly Application:

List the needs you want to submit to the Lord before you teach. Now, with an act of faith, submit those needs to him now, trusting and believing He will meet them.

Reread the scriptures below.
Jer. 29:11, THE MESSAGE
Gen. 50:20, THE MESSAGE
2 Pet. 1:3-4, THE MESSAGE

Write the principle (s) from the scriptures you find will be most useful to you as you teach.

Reflection/Notes:

LOVE IN YOUR CLASSROOM

1. **Read the Scriptures.**
    1 Cor. 1:7-9, THE MESSAGE
    1 Cor. 13:4-8, THE MESSAGE
2. **Read this week's teaching on love in your classroom.**

Love in Your Classroom. Too many today walk around in search of love. Too many are willing to give up the innermost parts of themselves just to experience love. Some will sacrifice family, themselves, and even their children in hopes of capturing the intangible—love. There is nothing wrong with wanting to be loved; it is human nature and one of our most basic needs. It is attached to our need to be accepted; it is attached to our willingness to accept; it is the essence of belonging to someone or to a family. The problem is many fall in love with the idea of love, but do not have a biblical understanding of what love is, so the search continues for an ideal of which they do not even have the true definition.

Understand that seeking love and acceptance from people—be it family, husband, wife, children—and reciprocating love to such people without having the love of Christ will surely fail. Having love for teaching without having love for Christ is a recipe for disaster. It is through Christ's love that we find love in our profession and for one another.

As educators, we are responsible for establishing an atmosphere of love in our classrooms and show students how to love others through our acts of love for them. 1 Cor. 13:4-8 is the love chapter and Paul breaks down the actions of love that we ought to be practicing.

Not only are we to be loved with patience, we are to be patient when loving. Not only are we not to exhibit a proud or envious nature when receiving love, we are not to do so when giving love. We are to honor one another and not keep a checklist of faults at our disposal to use against the other. Love trusts, protects, hopes, and always triumphs. To create a learning atmosphere exhibiting each of these characteristics of love, we must have a relationship with Jesus Christ. It takes His power and faith to love the unlovable beyond faults. Many students today suffer from anxiety, depression, stress, neglect and face many other challenges. The learning atmosphere of our classrooms must be one that calms, not exacerbates, these current challenges our students face.

We are only true agents of love if we have a relationship with Jesus Christ. When you love Him, he empowers you to love others; to exude love with words, actions, decisions, behaviors, thoughts, and overall treatment of others. Let your students witness God's love through your interactions with them showing them you will not give up on them because God will not give up on them (1 Cor. 1:7-9).

Weekly Application:

As an educator, you are called to love like Christ in the workplace, but you will need His help to do so. Christ's love will help you to love your students as He loves you. As you teach, teach with the love of Christ forgiving easily and repenting quickly.

Reread the scriptures below.
> 1 Cor. 1:7-9, THE MESSAGE
> 1 Cor. 13:4-8, THE MESSAGE

Write the principle (s) from the scriptures you find will be most useful to you as you teach.

Reflection/Notes:

ETHICS IN TEACHING

1. **Read the Scriptures.**
   MIC. 6:8, THE MESSAGE
   Prov. 6:16-19, THE MESSAGE
2. **Read this week's teaching on ethics in teaching.**

E thics in Teaching. Ethics has varying degrees of meaning for many and although worded differently, the consensus is the same. Ethics entails living with the guidance of a moral compass and gauging one's conduct by it.

In a post-modernist education culture, the temptation to rationalize lurks at each corner of the educator's conscience. When motivated by self, temptation dwarfs the educator's previously established ethical code resulting in compromise. So, as educators, we must continue to take stock of our own moral compass, and the rationalizations that might compromise our ethics, using what the Lord says as our barometer. He established right from wrong since before mankind's inception providing an ethical blueprint for us all.

He has shown us what to do, how to live and love, and gave the expectations for us (Mic. 6:8, THE MESSAGE). In God's eyes, there are six behaviors He hates including arrogance, lies, and confusion, (Prov.

6:16-19, THE MESSAGE) that stand to coerce educators to compromise their ethics.

While we know to be ethical, deciding and actually being ethical are two different things, but as educators, we must decide to be ethical and then actually be ethical. One can assess the true nature of an individual by what he does, not what he says. Consequently, our students assess our ethical nature by our actions, which makes it even more important to strive daily to maintain an ethical standard. Educators have an ethical capacity, in which they teach, that include honesty and intellect; they have a responsibility to their students, colleagues, administrators, and themselves to maintain them. In the same vein, we cannot be coerced by parents, students, colleagues, or administrators to compromise our ethical standards for promotions, salary increases, or students' academic benefit.

Following His blueprint outlined in Mic. 6:8 and Prov. 6:16-19 as closely as humanly possible is important in our efforts here. The eyes of the Lord are everywhere; there is nowhere we can go or anything we say or do that He will not know about. He knows it before it happens. He asks us to strive to do His will daily and He will do the rest. The scriptures give a command and require our execution, which guarantees divine interference, to help us maintain ethics in teaching.

Weekly Application:

As you teach, it is pertinent to maintain an ethical standard. Students are watching. Colleagues are watching. God is watching. Evaluate your ethical standard using Mic. 6:8 and Prov. 6:16-19. Verbally submit those areas of weakness to God in prayer believing, by faith, He will perfect them as you strive to maintain an ethical standard in teaching.

Reread the scriptures below.
> Mic. 6:8, THE MESSAGE
> Prov. 6:16-19, THE MESSAGE

Write the principle (s) from the scriptures you find will be most useful to you as you teach.

Reflection/Notes:

CHILDREN OF GOD

1. **Read the Scriptures.**
   Matt. 2:16-18, THE MESSAGE
   Jer. 1:5, THE MESSAGE
2. **Read this week's teaching on the children of God.**

Children of God. Children are precious beings God sees fit to bestow upon the world. He bestows them upon the world because children have a purpose too. Their purpose does not wait to materialize when they become adults. Their purpose is materialized before their conception. God knew them before they were formed in their mother's womb (Jer. 1:5). God has planned their entire lives from birth to death and has done so with purpose. So, the mere fact that they are sitting before you in your classroom is not by coincidence. It is by purpose. You have been divinely designated as one of those in the network of people God has ordained in your students' lives to help them arrive at their purpose.

It is the enemy's desire to derail students' divine purpose and kill it before it has a chance to materialize. He did it during the reign of King Herod. Matt. 2:16-18 tells of King Herod's plot to kill all the male babies including Jesus Christ to destroy the purpose God had for the children's lives especially Jesus. The enemy is still at work today, but you do not have to help him as King Herod did.

The enemy wants you to see your students as a nuisance, unworthy, hindrance, or as nothing. When you view your students unfavorably, you begin to lose hope in them and their future. You will also begin to treat your students the way you view them; slowly, students will begin to think unfavorably about themselves. There is a war for our generation of students. Many students welcome those who accept and positively affirm them instead of belittle, berate, and discourage them. The negative affirmations create an entry point for the enemy to derail them from their path to purpose. Your classroom is one of your students' pitstops on their way to their purpose. Be certain that they hear positive affirmations and correction in your classroom. At least in your classroom, the enemy will have no entry point. In your classroom, students will see and hear God in you. And while it may not appear to have an immediate impact on your students, the Lord will bring it back to their remembrance at the most opportune time because He knows their lives depend on it.

Having a relationship with God provides you the foundation you need to teach today's generation of students. Teaching can be an emotional rollercoaster. Your relationship with the Father balances your and your students' emotions. It also results in a stronger prayer life. and promotes frequent communion with God. A positive relationship with others—especially our students—happens effectively when we have a relationship with Him.

Weekly Application:

Before you teach, take the time to strengthen your relationship with the Lord byway of prayer and frequent communion with Him. He will equip you with discernment to know how to shape the future and minds of your students with your words.

Reread the scriptures below.
  Matt. 2:16-18, THE MESSAGE
  Jer. 1:5, THE MESSAGE

Write the principle (s) from the scriptures you find will be most useful to you as you teach.

Reflection/Notes:

THE ULTIMATE SECURITY

1. **Read the Scriptures.**
   2 Thess. 3:3, THE MESSAGE
   Pslm. 127:1, THE MESSAGE
   Deut. 31:6, THE MESSAGE
2. **Read this week's teaching on the ultimate security.**

T he Ultimate Security. Security means to provide protection for the one you are assigned to secure. The characteristics of the word security include providing a measure to guard against espionage or sabotage, crime, attack, or escape and any form of danger. Naturally, security is placed in shopping malls, museums, banks, and schools. Security surrounds celebrities, politicians, and even extends to buildings and commercial and personal property. The whole idea of security is to protect and offer a sense of freedom to those you were assigned to secure with the use of natural defense mechanisms. The freedom to live, work, and socialize.

Lately, however, the natural defense mechanisms, in their current condition, need support. Notable school violence is on the rise byway of school shootings and physical altercations. Students are dying and being injured at the hands of guns and one another. As the first line of defense for your students in your classroom, certainly, this makes some educators apprehensive about teaching in naturally unsecured schools.

To strengthen the natural security efforts in our schools, there are talks of staffing them with increased resource officers and installing metal detectors on campuses. While these efforts are applauded, without the ultimate security, the Chief Watchman provides, these efforts are in vain (Pslm. 127:1). We must invite the presence of our Spiritual security as well.

We need the presence of our resource officers and even metal detectors on our campuses, but without an increased presence of the Lord, these efforts are in vain.

The Spiritual security is the presence of the Lord. As an educator, you can invite His presence onto your campus and into your classroom before you enter your classroom.

Invite His presence to secure you first byway of prayer and relationship everywhere your feet treads. Next, anchor your trust in Him to secure you (2 Thess. 3:3, THE MESSAGE). Finally, be confident that, in your assignment to teach, your ultimate security is provided (Deut. 31:6, THE MESSAGE). He is there to protect at all times, but troubled times are not the only times we are invited to call on Him. Train your heart and mind to obey Deut. 31:6 and 2 Thess. 3:3). Do not be overcome with fear, doubt, and anxiety. Instead, rely on His security.

Weekly Application:

As you teach, denounce the spirit of fear and invoke the presence and protection of the Lord by saying aloud His promises from 2 Thess. 3:3 and Deut. 31:6. Repeat as often as necessary.

Reread the scriptures below.
2 Thess. 3:3, THE MESSAGE
Pslm. 127:1, THE MESSAGE
Deut. 31:6, THE MESSAGE

Write the principle (s) from the scriptures you find will be most useful to you as you teach.

Reflection/Notes:

OFFENSELESS

1. **Read the Scriptures.**
   Matt. 23:11, THE MESSAGE
   Heb. 6:10, THE MESSAGE
   Js. 1:19, THE MESSAGE
2. **Read this week's teaching on offenseless.**

Offenseless. Offenses should not impede your role to teach, but oftentimes, educators allow offenses to affect their assignment. Negative feelings and emotions of blame, shame, and frustration begin to cloud their teaching decisions and abilities. Depending on the degree and frequency of the offense, many will abort the assignment and leave the profession. They will use it as a reason to quit. They will allow the offense to linger and build a nest of unforgiveness toward the offender—be it students, colleagues, administrators, or anyone else who was involved. When you harbor the offenses, you're blinded to the meaning that the offensive experience can produce. Conflicts and offenses will happen in the workplace, but the question becomes what do you do? I have three recommendations for you.

1) Know who you work for.

Col. 3:23. You are to perform your tasks unto God, not man. You are not teaching as a favor for any one person, but you are being obedient to God. You were divinely placed as an educator and remaining true to your task means you are remaining true to God. When you remember these truths, you will continue to teach with your whole spiritual being and not out of your flesh basing it on how well, or bad, any one person treats you. Oftentimes, educators are the first to experience misdirected anger and frustration from others—especially our students. We spend the most time with them during the school year; we witness their high and low moments and ultimately, develop a stake in their well-being. Because we are there most of the time, we stand to be offended often, but it's our response to it that matters. When you find yourself in an offended emotional state, remember Col. 3:23.

2) Know that God remembers your work.

Heb. 6:10. He is not unjust. Your response to the offense is your test and not that of the offender. He will remember your work done in love unto His people. Yes, your students are children of God. They belong to Him too. Still do good work. God remembers.

3) Know to be patient, slow to speak, and quick to listen.

Js. 1:19. You will desire immediate reprimand for the offender in your various situations, but be patient. God will administer judgment to the offender; Lk. 17:1 reminds us that woe will be unto those who deliver offenses to another. Your moment of conflict and offense will require patience. Trust the Lord to speak for you; to vindicate you; and you continue to teach.

Weekly Application:

As you teach, know who you work for, be patient, slow to speak, and quick to listen, and know that God remembers your work. Do not harbor the offense.

Reread the scriptures below.
    Matt. 23:11, THE MESSAGE
    Heb. 6:10, THE MESSAGE
    Js. 1:19, THE MESSAGE

Write the principle (s) from the scriptures you find will be most useful to you as you teach.

Reflection/Notes:

WEEK 14

SPEAK

1. **Read the Scriptures.**
   1 Cor. 14:33, THE MESSAGE
   Mrk. 9:25-29, THE MESSAGE
2. **Read this week's teaching on speak.**

Speak. One action item on the enemy's agenda is to silence educators. Silencing your voice in your students' lives, aids his efforts to derail their future. Are you an educator who teaches passively? Have you pacified your instructional style with excuses—I don't feel like teaching today or I will not teach until I get a raise? When you allow these feelings to dictate how and whether you teach, the enemy is attacking your voice.

Your voice is not only a portal of information. Your voice is power. It is used to release blessings over your and your students' lives releasing the hold of bondage and negativity. It is used to speak dreams into existence. It is used to uplift, empower, and inspire. It is used to speak God's Word and decrees. If the enemy can manipulate you to not use your voice, you'll never experience the true power of it for yourself or your students. He can continue to wreak havoc in every area of your and your students' lives. Through his agents, the enemy wants to silence you. He knows the power of your voice, but its important to recognize the power in your voice as well. Our voice commands, praises, delivers, blesses, directs, and educates. When we speak, our words are released into the atmosphere to achieve one or more of these purposes. In Mrk. 9:25, Jesus demonstrates the power in speaking before an entire crowd.

²⁵ When Jesus saw that the crowd of onlookers was growing, he rebuked the evil[a] spirit. "Listen, you spirit that makes this boy unable to hear and speak," he said. "I command you to come out of this child and never enter him again!" –Mark 9:25, NLT. Jesus' demonstration confirms that speechless spirits exist and that they can be cast out.

The speechless spirit does not discriminate against age, race, gender, or any other categorical construct, which means it can attack you as an educator. As surely as you teach, the enemy will make an attempt to silence you. Do not give way to his speechless spirit. Reaffirm control over your voice and yield it to the Spirit of God. Mrk. 9:28-29 shares the instruction.

²⁸ Afterward, when Jesus was alone in the house with his disciples, they asked him, "Why couldn't we cast out that evil spirit?" ²⁹ Jesus replied, "This kind can be cast out only by prayer." Praying is the only way to rid yourself of the speechless spirit. There are enough voices seeking to spiritually assassinate the purpose for our students' future, but your voice does not have to be one of them. Remember its capabilities and ensure to yield your voice to God.

Weekly Application:

As you teach, reaffirm your voice as power through prayer. Pray to ward of the speechless spirit to free yourself from its efforts to close your mouth and ears to knowledge, freedom, and blessings for you and your students.

Reread the scriptures below.
   1 Cor. 14:33, THE MESSAGE
   Mrk. 9:25-29, THE MESSAGE

Write the principle (s) from the scriptures you find will be most useful to you as you teach.

Reflection/Notes:

GOOD DAYS VS. BAD DAYS

1. **Read the Scriptures.**
    Pslm. 118:24, THE MESSAGE
    Jhn. 16:33, THE MESSAGE
    Jb. 2:10, THE MESSAGE
2. **Read this week's teaching on good days vs. bad days.**

G ood Days vs. Bad Days. No two days, months, weeks, or years will be alike. No one, arguably, in the Bible realized this more than Job. As God's most righteous servant, Job experienced the best God had to offer. He had good health, family, business, and he was the most influential man in all the East (Job 1:12). The children were successful also. He was a blessed man who enjoyed the goodness of his days that God provided. Until he lost it all in one day. You might say Job was having more than a just a bad day. What's equally important, however, is Job's response to his bad day.

On our bad days, it's possible to think God's presence is not with us otherwise He would have prevented the trouble, right? Wrong. We know we will have trouble because Jesus warns us that we will (Jhn. 16:33). But he also admonishes us to take heart because he has overcome the world and this includes the trouble in it too (Jhn. 16:33).

Job experiences the good and bad and reminds us that we cannot take His good days and not the bad (Jb. 2:10). Everyday is a gift from Him and we must rejoice in each day (Pslm. 118:24) growing through the experiences each one brings.

As an educator, your days will vary. Sometimes your lesson will go as planned for each class with full cooperation from your students. Other days, your students will be moody, unresponsive, uncooperative, disrespectful or simply disinterested. Other days, you might realize you were overzealous in planning your lesson plan. These days are not indications that you're not teaching well or that God's presence is not with you. This is an indication that you are to lean more on God's promises. He promises to never leave you (Heb. 13:5). It is He who changes the heart of people (Prov. 21:1) and yes, these people include students. It is God's promises that give the revelation of who you are and your purpose everyday. Your bad days do not change any of these truths.

Although Job had the counsel of his three friends, it was his prayer that invoked God's presence. You too will have the counsel of your veteran educators and the knowledge of pedagogy and classroom management techniques. But no matter how much truth and advice are given to you, none of its implementations will be fruitful without God's presence to help you discern their counsel and whether it aligns with His promises.

Weekly Application:

As you teach, discern worldly counsel from Godly counsel and implement the latter in your teaching practices daily. Lean on His promises.

Reread the scriptures below.
   Pslm. 118:24, THE MESSAGE
   Jhn. 16:33, THE MESSAGE
   Jb. 2:10, THE MESSAGE

Write the principle (s) from the scriptures you find will be most useful to you as you teach.

Reflection/Notes:

ME, MYSELF, AND I

1. **Read the Scriptures.**
    Mrk. 12:31, THE MESSAGE
    Jhn. 5:19, THE MESSAGE
2. **Read this week's teaching on me, myself, and I.**

M e, Myself, and I. Inherent in Jhn. 5:19-20, Jesus offers two important acts we should execute daily. Me, myself, and I scream
independence. It is a mantra many have adopted to assert autonomy in
their lives, finances, profession, and relationships. Independence is not
necessarily a poor trait to have, but misunderstanding it is. A misunderstanding of independence can lead to pride and self-reliance, which is the
perfect set-up for a fall.

Independence has varying degrees of meaning, but at its core, independence means simply not relying on another person or entity for any
type of support; thus, by this definition, one who becomes independent is
reliant upon him or herself.

As an educator, you cannot place ultimate trust in our ability to teach,
discipline, and counsel. Jhn. 5:19, Jesus tells that he [as the Son] cannot
operate independent of the Father. In other words, he could not heal,

deliver, feed multitudes, or even teach without full dependence on the Father. Herein lies the first step for educators.

Place what you think your talents and abilities are in God's hands; acknowledge daily that your strengths come from him and nothing or anyone else; finally, thank him for it. With the many accolades you receive for your efforts, you will be tempted to assume the credit, but do not succumb to a common character flaw of mankind-pride. The second step can be found in that same verse.

Jesus imitates his Father's behaviors. As educators, our role models should be other educators and administrators who also imitate our heavenly Father's behaviors.

Jesus imitates the Father

You imitate Jesus.

Thus, imitating Jesus, imitates the Father,
illustrating His goodness.

Jesus' success in his life came as a direct result of his obedience to the Father. For in God lies wisdom, authority, foresight, insight, and revelation. If Jesus needed to rely on God for his mental aptitude, we certainly do as educators. In relying on the Father for his very existence, Jesus imitated His ways. Jhn. 5:19 tells us that he first can do nothing apart from the Father and secondly, he only does what He has seen the Father do. When imitating goodness, your results will be fruitful and prosperous.

Weekly Application:

As you teach, let your students see you imitating Jesus; your behaviors imitating Jesus; your instructional style imitating Jesus; and your interaction with them imitating Jesus.

Reread the scriptures below.
   Mrk. 12:31, THE MESSAGE
   Jhn. 5:19, THE MESSAGE

Write the principle (s) from the scriptures you find will be most useful to you as you teach.

Reflection/Notes:

WALK IT OUT

1. **Read the Scriptures.**
   TI. 1:7-8, THE MESSAGE
2. **Read this week's teaching on walking it out.**

Walk it Out. Much is required of today's educators. We not only serve as educators, but float in the roles of counselors, role models, advisors, and sometimes, a parental figure as well. Students look to us for education, but some will look to us for more—to be cultured or educated and refined in the ways of life. They want to see what we can teach them also about life. In our approach, we must be far from venal, but operate with the utmost integrity in our classrooms. Our students are watching and listening.

In his instructions to Titus, the Apostle Paul tells him to appoint elders with integrity to oversee the house and people of God. These people were entrusted to the elders and therefore had to illustrate a principled lifestyle for the people would be watching and listening. Your position as an educator is similar to that of the designated elders. As the people were entrusted to them, your students are entrusted to you.

Each selected elder had to be blameless, not overbearing, quick tempered, alcoholics, violent, or venal. (v.7). They needed to be hospitable, loving, welcoming, upright, self-controlled, and disciplined (v. 8). As the elders possessed the spiritual and leadership qualities to oversee the people, you possess both to oversee your students. Embodying these characteristics allowed the truth of sound doctrine to be taught and not echo the lies and false teachings of the Cretans.

God has appointed you to oversee your students according to the same criteria. As an educator, you set the tone of your classrooms and you want to make sure it is not hypocritical before Him or your students. Not only will you need to be mindful of your behavior in the classroom, but you will need to mind it beyond the classroom. Off the clock, your lifestyle should also be sincere and reflective of God's criteria much like the appointed Elders.

Living an integral life will ensure you teach and exhibit integrity, which is what today's students need to see. You will show them that you are well-versed in your discipline and lifestyle. Embodying the characteristics in v. 8 shows your students that there is a standard at school, in your classroom, and your life.

Weekly Application:

As you teach, be the hospitable, loving, welcoming, upright, self-controlled, and disciplined (v. 8) elder in your classroom through your actions, decisions, and speech. When in doubt, check each by God's standard in scripture.

Reread the scriptures below.

Ti. 1:7-8, THE MESSAGE

Write the principle (s) from the scriptures you find will be most useful to you as you teach.

Reflection/Notes:

THE CALL

1. **Read the Scriptures.**
    1 Cor.1: 1-2, THE MESSAGE
    Mrk. 1:17, THE MESSAGE
2. **Read this week's teaching on the call.**

The Call. When Jesus walked along the sea of Galilee, Simon (Peter) and his brother Andrew were performing the task of jobs as fisherman merely casting their net into the lake expecting a harvest of fish. However, as he just walked by and saw them, he gave them a command and a new assignment.

Like Simon and his brother, the Father has gifted us with skills and talents to be used to make a living and create wealth. At the same time, he intends for those same skills and talents to be used to carry out His will in our lives as well. The latter only materializes once we obey the first command—come follow me [Jesus]. When we commit to following Jesus, like Simon and his brother, we can be sure that he will assign purpose. Without Jesus, they were merely fisherman. With him, they became complicit in his assignment to win souls for God's Kingdom. They became his disciples. Both brothers dropped their nets and followed Jesus. Mrk 1:17.

First came the call and then came the command to make them fishers of men, which equates to winning souls to Christ. Their skills were no longer simply good enough for their well-being, but it was now being used for Kingdom purpose. The brothers accepted the call, obeyed the command, and went on to win many souls to Christ.

As educators, God is calling you to follow him and use your natural ability to teach in His way to also win souls to Christ. As the Apostle Paul undoubtedly knew his call for his purpose (1 Cor.1: 1-2) and Simon and Andrew knew their call to walk with Jesus, you will know your call is to teach for this season in your life.

Weekly Application:

As you teach, attune your spiritual senses to the call to become fishers of men in your classroom. In His leading, you may be prompted during a student-teacher conference, advising, or counseling meeting session to introduce a student to Christ.

Reread the scriptures below.
    1 Cor.1: 1-2, THE MESSAGE
    Mrk. 1:17, THE MESSAGE

Write the principle (s) from the scriptures you find will be most useful to you as you teach.

Reflection/Notes:

STEAL AWAY

1. **Read the Scriptures.**
    Lk. 5:16, THE MESSAGE
    Mrk. 1:35, THE MESSAGE
2. **Read this week's teaching on steal away.**

Steal Away. With faculty and staff meetings, conferences and teaching, educators' days are usually filled every waking minute they're at work. Sometimes, you barely have time to take a lunch break or a potty break. You may find yourself overwhelmed by the task of the day and the energy expended to complete them leaving you craving a private moment to yourself. It is in these moments that Jesus wants you to know he is there in the chaos and invite you to steal away to him.

During his ministry, Jesus carefully illustrated the art and practice of private prayer (Lk. 5:16). His private prayer moments were the source of his strength, power, direction, and most of all, peace. He did not allow teaching extensively in the temple and before the crowds outside of the temple to substitute for his private prayer time. In fact, his task showed him how much he needed private prayer to regain his footing and strength to continue in his assignment and purpose. As an educator, you will need to do the same.

When you find that your day is becoming too busy and you begin to feel overwhelmed, steal away to the power source through prayer. Pray for yourself, students, administrators, and colleagues to regain your footing for your day. We are invited to commune with him anytime and anywhere; he welcomes us. We do not have to confine our prayers to him to our homes, cars, or even church. You can steal away in your office or classroom. When you steal away, you make the space to quiet your thoughts and calm your spirit in the midst of your teaching, grading, managing, disciplining, and conferencing.

Weekly Application:

As you teach, be attuned to your mind, body, and spirit and recognize when you need to steal away to be refreshed and revived at any point during your teaching day.

Reread the scriptures below.
  Lk. 5:16, THE MESSAGE
  Mrk. 1:35, THE MESSAGE

Write the principle (s) from the scriptures you find will be most useful to you as you teach.

Reflection/Notes:

BE THE LIGHT

1. **Read the Scriptures.**
   Jhn. 8:12, THE MESSAGE
   Mrk. 4:21, THE MESSAGE
2. **Read this week's teaching on being the light.**

B e the Light. We are the light. The light is within us. That light must shine at all times. Yet, when many of us go to work, we shut off our light; we steer clear of faith and education when Jesus has given us the power to trample over serpents and scorpions. He does not want us to only shine our light at home, in the church, or at Bible Study, he wants us to shine it everywhere—even in the workplace.

What is the light? The light is the Gospel of Jesus Christ. The light is the love and goodness of God. The light is the love of Jesus. The light is the truth of Jesus. As a committed vessel unto him, he uses you as the conduit of his light, which means your light may be to provide compassion, aid, resources, assistance, love, empathy, or sympathy to those who may need it on any given day. As the light, we are asked to place Jesus' purpose over our needs in order to dispel the darkness in some else's life.

In Mrk. 4:21, Jesus asked them who finds the light? Who shields it from the view of others? When you recognize his light within you, and you intentionally hide it, it is offensive to Jesus and to you. The light radiates positivity. The light heals and soothes the carrier and those the carrier encounters. On any given day, our students will need to experience that light that you radiate.

When we follow Jesus, we walk in the light (Jhn. 8:12). We are emboldened and empowered when we have his light. His light gives us optimistic eyes to view our students, colleagues, administrators, and ourselves. Without his light, our efforts to teach and invoke change in the lives of those we encounter are futile. It is his light that makes the difference in us and in our interactions with others.

Weekly Application:

As you teach, shine your light every day in your classroom. Light dispels darkness and awakens a spirit of vitality in those around us. Let the light of Jesus that overtakes you overtake those in your presence today.

Reread the scriptures below.
Jhn. 8:12, THE MESSAGE
Mrk. 4:21, THE MESSAGE

Write the principle (s) from the scriptures you find will be most useful to you as you teach.

Reflection/Notes:

Teaching From Your Heart

1. **Read the Scriptures.**
   Jer. 17:9, THE MESSAGE
   Jhn. 2:25, THE MESSAGE
   Prov. 4:23, THE MESSAGE
2. **Read this week's teaching on teaching from the heart.**

Teaching From Your Heart. Educators teach from the heart and not the book is a quote plastered to my desk. While this is true, the heart from which we teach matters equally as much. For what flows from our mouths lines up with what is in our hearts. From our hearts, flows the issues of life (Prov. 4:23). If the issues of our lives remain unresolved, what flows from our hearts to our mouths will confirm those unresolved issues in our lives. As educators, it is not good enough to simply teach from our hearts, but we must teach from the heart that Jesus transforms.

Our hearts are desperately wicked, beyond natural measure, and no human being can know it (Jer. 17:9). While our intentions may be good toward students, colleagues, and administrators, the true nature of hearts will dictate whether they truly are good. The good news is you don't have the isolate the condition of your heart to you. Jesus knows your heart and wants to transform it. He says there is no need to testify to him about any man because he knows what is in every man (Jhn. 2:25) including you. It is in your best interest to surrender your heart to him. He can mold it, so it is genuinely good.

When we teach with a transformed heart, we are sure to obey his commands and love. We will first be truthful in our dedication and love for Him in our daily lives and then to those we encounter. We can submit our spirit to him and be obedient to His word (truth), so the Son and Father will abide in us. It is a transformed heart that allows us to love and wills us to obey. With their presence, you can be confident in the love you show to your students, colleagues, and administrators. You can be purposeful in prayer, not praying about the issues another has within him or herself or about another person. You can be strategic in your professional and personal approaches with others relying on the Spirit to steer you in His direction to achieve purpose.

Weekly Application:

As you teach, pray to the Lord and ask Him to renew your heart; to give you a heart of flesh that radiates true love and obedience to Him and others.

Reread the scriptures below.
> Jer. 17:9, THE MESSAGE
> Jhn. 2:25, THE MESSAGE
> Prov. 4:23, THE MESSAGE

Write the principle (s) from the scriptures you find will be most useful to you as you teach.

Reflection/Notes:

THE RIGHT WAY

1. **Read the Scriptures.**
   Rom. 13:1, THE MESSAGE
   Philip. 2:14, THE MESSAGE
2. **Read this week's teaching on the right way.**

The Right Way. Educators, not only will you want your students to adhere to such caution, but you want to do the same. You want to do *it* the right way. What is *it*? What is *the right way? It* is your job and all responsibilities associated with it.

I recall the first two years of teaching were probationary. During these two years, new educators undergo a new faculty training and development. After being fresh out of graduate school, having completed practicums, master's thesis, and other research projects, I did not care to participate in any additional trainings. Armed with my degrees and pedagogical techniques, all I wanted to do was teach. Some of you educators can relate. Nothing wrong with my desire, right?

As an educator, you will be given much instruction and many tasks. The question becomes how will you do the tasks set before you? Will you perform them with murmurings of discontent? Or will you do the exact opposite? Will you adhere to the instructions given or rewrite them to your liking? Will you do it *the right way*?

Philip. 2:14 *explains the right way*, which means to perform your tasks humbly and pleasantly. Our attitude determines our aptitude not only in life, but also in Christ. When we humble ourselves before our superiors, we are humbling ourselves before the Lord because we are to obey those who have rule over us (Rom. 13:1). Moreso, we are setting an example for our students and colleagues. Although I believed the new faculty training subtracted time from teaching and mentoring, I participated. Accepting the position confirmed my willingness to perform my job and all responsibilities associated with it. Accepting my call from God to teach confirmed my willingness to obey His word. And in His Word, he says to obey my boss (Rom. 13:1). So, I did. It is easy and tempting to vehemently rebel and invite others to join us in our rebellion. It is more challenging to obey and execute with a smile. The latter is more rewarding.

Weekly Application:

As you teach, commit to maintaining a positive attitude and exuding a spirit of cooperation when performing your tasks. Pray for God to help you maintain your commitment.

Reread the scriptures below.
   Rom. 13:1, THE MESSAGE
   Philip. 9: 2:14, THE MESSAGE

Write the principle (s) from the scriptures you find will be most useful to you as you teach.

Reflection/Notes:

ASK FOR IT

1. **Read the Scriptures.**
   Matt. 7:7, THE MESSAGE
   Philip. 4:6, THE MESSAGE
2. **Read this week's teaching on ask for it.**

Ask for It. Usually, I spend the night before my class reviewing my lesson plans and making changes as needed to accommodate my student learning outcomes. As an educator, we are often given multiple courses which make for multiple preps, so I tried to always be prepared. I would arrive two hours before class even began. I wanted to make sure I had copies of handouts for students, course materials, and working technology in my classroom. I also wanted some time to review the readings associated with my lecture for the day.

When I thought I had an exceptional lesson, I would hardly sleep the night before. I was eagerly anticipating the day and the students' response to the lesson. Now, rarely will your students ever be as excited as you about the lesson—just remember that. I, however, at least anticipated the lesson garnering more excitement than it usually did.

All went well until one of my classes responded negatively to the lesson. I could not understand why they refused to cooperate and asked irrelevant questions. The educator within me wanted to stick to the teaching points on the lesson plan I had so thoroughly prepared. Later in my teaching years, I learned to flow with the students and use these uncooperative and intuitive moments as teaching moments. But that was hardly my focus on this day.

The reaction from that class made me so anxious about the same lesson for the next class that I sabotaged it. I addressed questions from the previous class that this current class had not asked. Because the students were confused by my approach, the lesson did not go well in this class either.

Although the lesson was well-planned, I did not submit it, and my expectations to Him in prayer. Phil. 4:6 reminds us to not to be anxious about anything; instead, submit our needs to him in prayer and supplication. There will be moments in your teaching day, and even before the teaching day begins, where anxieties will arise and even increase in intensity. That is the time to redirect your concerns to the One who can resolve them and offer new strategy and insight.

Any anxiety you may be feeling about your class or students today are not yours alone; you have support of the One who cares for your soul daily. Ask for it—ask for what you need to today (Matt.7:7).

Weekly Application:

Write down any anxieties you experience this week. Verbally submit them to the Lord and ask Him for what you need and rest peacefully knowing that he has already provided it for you.

Reread the scriptures below.
Matt. 7:7, THE MESSAGE
Philip. 4:6, THE MESSAGE

Write the principle (s) from the scriptures you find will be most useful to you as you teach.

Reflection/Notes:

WEEK 24

YOUR MIND?

1. **Read the Scriptures.**
   Philip. 4:8, THE MESSAGE
   2 Cor. 5:21, THE MESSAGE
   Philip. 4:9, THE MESSAGE
2. **Read this week's teaching on your mind.**

Your Mind. As an educator, you want to have a good professional rep-
utation, but not at the expense of your social values and beliefs. You
are not going to please everyone or make yourself happy all of the time,
so it is important to remain abreast of what you should think and focus
on daily as an educator to nourish your soul.

Words are important and being an educator opens your eyes to the
power of words. Words can encourage or discourage you. Words can
uplift or depress you. Words can bless or curse you. Most of the accolades
you will receive as an educator will be verbal, but you will receive criticisms the same way.

As an educator, do not focus on the negative or the criticisms you
will receive. You will make a mistake or a misstep; and even when you do
not, it is possible to be criticized because you did not yield to the requests
of your colleagues, students, or parents. We know this to be true because

Jesus, who was perfect and knew no sin, was criticized and chastised and accused (2 Cor. 5:21). How much more will it happen to us? Yet, he did not revile, so you are to put into practice what you have seen Him do. The Apostle Paul gives this instruction in (Philip. 4:9) and we can apply it to Jesus Christ as well.

Do not allow the negative words to establish residency in your mind. It will provide leverage for the enemy to manipulate your thoughts. Focus on the encouraging, uplifting, and blessing words spoken to you. And only receive and use sincere, constructive criticism to help you be a better person and educator.

Weekly Application:

As you teach, think on what is true, noble, and right. For every negative thought you have, replace it with a good thought by thinking on a compliment from a student, colleague, boss, friend, or even by reading an e-mail note sent with some kind words. Then, you make an extra effort to extend a kind word to your colleagues for the hard work they are doing as well.

Reread the scriptures below.
   Philip. 4:8, THE MESSAGE
   2 Cor. 5:21, THE MESSAGE
   Philip. 4:9, THE MESSAGE

Write the principle (s) from the scriptures you find will be most useful to you as you teach.

Reflection/Notes:

PUT ON A SMILE

1. **Read the Scriptures.**
   Is. 1:18, THE MESSAGE
   1 Jhn. 1:9, THE MESSAGE
   Is. 61:3, THE MESSAGE
2. **Read this week's teaching on put on a smile.**

P ut on a Smile. Having taught earlier in the afternoon, I noticed an overwhelming spirit of sadness and hopelessness looming over one of my students. His head hung low and he stood with a slumped posture. When he looked up, worry seemed to overshadow him. His infectious smile that motivated many students on any given day was merely nonexistent.

I was unsure whether he had been hurt or whether he had hurt another individual. I was sure, however, that God is a merciful and forgiving God. One of my favorite scriptures in the Old Testament is Is. 1:18 where the Lord welcomingly invites us in to reason together regarding our transgressions When we confess our sins, he is just to forgive them (1 Jhn. 1:9), which is what reason means here. In Is. 61:3, the Lord appointed the Prophet Isaiah to deliver the good news to them that He sees their pain and will not leave them.

While I did not know what was ailing my student, I was certain of three truths: 1.) God is forgiving. 2.) God wants to reason with us. 3.) We can rejoice because he will never leave us.

As an educator, you will need the wisdom to comfort some of your students during times of uncertainty and their emotional distress. Before I could encourage my student in the Lord, I had to have encouraged myself in the Lord (1 Sam. 30:6). I strongly encouraged my student to simply praise the Lord. Praise breaks the mold of heaviness and shows God we still believe in His favor and that He will comfort us.

Death, heartbreak, loneliness, family issues, academic and social challenges are but a few woes in life that can cloak students in a spirit of heaviness. It is important for you, as an educator, to know that the students do not have to accept their state of emotional distress. the circumstances of his sadness. For we know such things will come, but it is in Him that we can find our joy (Jhn. 16:33). When the spirit of heaviness attempts to suffocate your students' spirit, put on a smile and praise the Lord. Having experienced his joy, you can be confident in encouraging your students, or colleagues and administrators to do the same.

Weekly Application:

As you teach, be ever mindful of the heaviness students can experience. When the woes of life seem to cloak them in a spirit of heaviness, remind them of these truths. 1.) God is forgiving. 2.) God wants to reason with us. 3.) Rejoice because he will never leave us.

Reread the scriptures below.

    Is. 1:18, THE MESSAGE

    1 Jhn. 1:9, THE MESSAGE

    Is. 61:3, THE MESSAGE

Write the principle (s) from the scriptures you find will be most useful to you as you teach.

Reflection/Notes:

YOUR REWARD

1. **Read the Scriptures.**
   Col. 3:24, THE MESSAGE
2. **Read this week's teaching on your reward.**

Y our Reward. The teaching profession is just as competitive as sports. You find yourself fighting for promotions, fighting for a compliment on your good work, and fighting for awards and recognition for all the teaching you do. If you're not careful, it will become the driving force behind your teaching decisions. When the awards and accolades and recognition never come, you find yourself wondering what you were doing wrong and what you did wrong when the reality of it is you did nothing wrong. Some educators teach with the hopes that someone will take notice of what they do; you want to have a feeling of achievement or accomplishment.

I understand. Although I did a lot with service learning, extracurricular activities, committees, and served as lead English Faculty, I found myself doing them for the sake of getting rewarded for them; to receive a pat on the back for getting noticed for these things. When the accolades didn't come, I began to feel like coaching the quiz bowl team and organizing community activities, to name a few, did not matter.

Col. 3:24 reminds us to perform for the Master for when we work unto him, we are sure to receive our due reward, in due time, from him. As educators, we cannot make the mistake of pleasing parents, administrators, students, or even ourselves over him. I had forgotten about the students entrusted to my care; I became focused on my accomplishments as an educator. My heart's posture toward my assignment was arrogant and negligent.

Without the promotion and awards or the special recognition from colleagues or administrators, know that you always have it from God. It is Him for whom we work. He is watching to see how well we perform on our assignment. You are to do it with all of your talents and abilities He has gifted unto you even when your reward never comes from man.

Weekly Application:

When you go home for the day, do not go home wishing you would've gotten that pat on the back from your principal or your lead teacher or your department chair. Just make sure that you get a pat on the back from the Lord. When you do work unto Him, He is sure to be glorified and your students are sure to be edified and you are sure to be gratified at the end of the day.

Reread the scriptures below.
   Col. 3:24, THE MESSAGE

Write the principle (s) from the scriptures you find will be most useful to you as you teach.

Reflection/Notes:

ALL IN HIS NAME

1. Read the Scriptures.

   Col. 3:17, THE MESSAGE

2. Read this week's teaching on all in His name.

All in His Name. As an educator, your teaching assignment should not be modified according to whom you believe your audience is. However, we allow students' perception, perspective, and behavior to dictate how we teach them and what we teach them. When this happens, they now have become your audience.

I recall being assigned to teach a Dual Enrollment course of 30 high school students. Nothing against these precious souls. Faced with their disinterest in learning and dismissive attitude towards learning, I allowed it to determine my teaching style and content. Because my audience was no longer God, I began to subconsciously behave in the same immature manner that they were behaving. Bad choice. Why? Because they now became my audience dictating how and what I taught. When their attitude was good, I taught well. When it was not, students got a subpar lesson.

Col. 3:17 reminds us to do all things in the name of our Lord Jesus; not in the in the name of our students' behavior and attitudes. Keeping a perspective of your core audience will ensure you are at your best for each lesson. Teach in excellence each day.

Weekly Application:

Remember, you also teach for Him. No matter what your students do or don't do, how they respond or don't respond, you still teach as if you're teaching to him—because you are. It is on these days we want to especially remember to let his light within us shine for our students. Teach all in His name.

Reread the scriptures below.
   Col. 3:17, THE MESSAGE

Write the principle (s) from the scriptures you find will be most useful to you as you teach.

Reflection/Notes:

BIG THINGS

1. Read the Scriptures.

> **Prov. 11:17, THE MESSAGE**
>
> **Js. 3:5, THE MESSAGE**

2. Read this week's teaching on big things.

Big Things. Educators have the Spirit of love. We are unique. We do not see our students the way others see them. We see what they can be; we see them as future doctors, lawyers, presidents, and politicians. As an educator, you are teaching the student your student will become. Using your tongue, you have the power to speak words of transformation in the lives of your students no matter what they may have been exposed to in their lives before meeting you.

One of my students delivered a motivational speech before the class and used his Uncle, a former criminal once featured on *American Greed*, as an example of how he thought he wanted to live—a luxurious lifestyle made possible byway of thievery. Sometimes students are exposed to negativity byway of their family and upbringing. Simply being in a wayward environment can serve as a negative affirmation. The question becomes— will they receive the same negative affirmations from you?

Many times, you will be the only voice of confidence, motivation, or perhaps even encouragement some of your students will hear. In each day, during each lesson, use your tongue to not only speak words of instruction, but also to uplift their spirits and transform their current perception of themselves into one that is greater than they can imagine.

Let your words be the arrows that pierce their intellect slowly killing any negative thoughts and affirmations they may have received throughout their lives. Let your words speak life unto their goals and spirit. Speak big things into the lives of your students and watch them flourish like a budding flower, right before your very eyes.

Weekly Application:

As you teach, be intentional in using words to affirm and uplift your students. Speak blessings into their life; strength when they appear weary; and motivations where they appear to be absent. Do not worry if the student does not receive your words at this time. Rest assured they will remember your kind words in the days to come.

Reread the scriptures below.
  Prov. 11:17, THE MESSAGE
  Js. 3:5, THE MESSAGE

Write the principle (s) from the scriptures you find will be most useful to you as you teach.

Reflection/Notes:

GOD CONNECTION

1. **Read the Scriptures.**
   Matt. 6:4, THE MESSAGE
   Prov. 18:24, THE MESSAGE
2. **Read this week's teaching on God Connection.**

G od Connection. A connection denotes a relationship between things and people. The efforts of each party in that relationship are what make it publicly and privately successful. As an educator, you will develop connections with your students, colleagues, administrators, parents, and the community. But the success of your public relationships with them is contingent upon the success of your private relationship with God.

For natural relationships to be successful, they require time and dedication at minimum. The same holds true for a relationship with God. A relationship denotes stability, security, reliance, help, and love and is usually established with another who can provide these for us. Blood is thicker than water often denotes the closeness that families share with another. Perhaps this is why the proverbs choose to describe God's relationship with us through the context of family.

Prov. 18:24 reminds us of a friend who sticks closer than a brother and that relying on the unreliable is sure to end in failure. As an educator, you have, or will make, numerous connections with colleagues, students, parents, professionals, and the community to say the least. The key to a successful relationship with each of them is to build a successful relationship with God. Many of those people will serve your professional and educational needs, but do not make the mistake of placing sole reliance upon your connection with them. It is the God connection that makes your other connections successful.

He rewards us openly for what is done in secret (Matt. 6:4). When you pray and worship Him in private, you are cultivating a relationship with Him, which is what you will need to be effective in your role as an educator.

Weekly Application:

As you teach, look for the God connection in your life and then pinpoint them in the other connections in your life. A strong private God connection can ensure a strong public connection with Him and others.

Reread the scriptures below.
Matt: 6:4, THE MESSAGE
Prov. 18:24, THE MESSAGE

Write the principle (s) from the scriptures you find will be most useful to you as you teach.

Reflection/Notes:

DISCIPLE

1. **Read the Scriptures.**
     Mrk. 16:15, THE MESSAGE
     Matt. 25:40, THE MESSAGE
2. **Read this week's teaching on disciple.**

D isciple. Yes. Educators are one of the most hardest working professionals, but yet, still underpaid and unappreciated. Teacher strikes and walkouts happen across the country because educators need their concerns to be heard and rightfully so. However, educators have been called to do more than teach; they have been called to disciple.

We see a pattern of discipleship throughout the Bible. Moses and Joshua. Elijah and Elisha. Naomi and Ruth. Jesus and his disciples are the ultimate example of discipleship. As their teacher, Jesus understood their weaknesses and shortcomings. He understood their limitations and although frustrating at times, Jesus never rejected his calling to disciple. In his ministry, he discipled for three years and did not abandon it at any time for any reason.

Keep in mind, quite a few circumstances arose that would have, for some, probably justified Jesus' decision, had he made it, to abandon the call. Yet, Jesus knew the purpose in his calling. He also knew what was at stake—the salvation of mankind. In the same way, educators, if you continue to be distracted by all the factors that lead to the teacher strikes, you may risk forfeiting the educational salvation of your students. It is the students who lose as a result of our temporary or permanent abandonment.

So, undoubtedly it is challenging for an educator in today's society—mediocre compensation, overcrowded classrooms, and inadequate resources. Educators serve in multiple capacities and it is not easy. I encourage you to endure the hardness for a greater cause. God has you in that position at that school for a purpose. There is a person or a group you have been assigned to disciple for that season in your life.

In these tough moments, as you teach, find your garden of Gethsemane and pray for God's will to be done for the time you are there. He will send an Angel to encourage and strengthen you to fulfill your task. Be watchful. Your Angel could be a colleague, student, stranger, mentor, or another unlikely source.

Weekly Application:

As you teach, follow the leading of the Lord to learn how to disciple those you may encounter. He will reveal strategies to you throughout your teaching days.

Reread the scriptures below.
   Mrk. 16:15, THE MESSAGE
   Matt. 25:40, THE MESSAGE

Write the principle (s) from the scriptures you find will be most useful to you as you teach.

Reflection/Notes:

LEAN NOT ON YOU

1. **Read the Scriptures.**
   Is. 55:8, THE MESSAGE
   Rev.1:8, THE MESSAGE
   Prov. 3:5-7, THE MESSAGE
2. **Read this week's teaching on it is well.**

Lean Not on You. Naturally, we rely on what we can see. Our reliance has come to be upon ourselves, money, education, and people. We look to them for encouragement, help, advice, and so on. While these resources can provide the answer and help we need, we are encouraged to not lean on our own understanding to get there.

You will have many questions throughout your teaching career ranging from teaching duties to the best way to structure parent and student teacher conferences to resolving conflicts with both parties. Teacher education programs train educators as well as possible, but experience in the classroom will be your ultimate teacher. As you learn from your experience in the classroom, remember a proverb from the wisest man to have ever lived.

King Solomon, son of David and King of the Israelites, admonishes us to seek understanding from God first and not ourselves. His reason is simple. When we seek understanding, we seek direction, advice, help, and knowledge in an effort to make the best decision possible. Starting with God first is best as He knows the roads we are to and will take as well as the outcome of each one. In the words of King Solomon, he will make our paths straight (v.6).

A lack of understanding can create a hindrance, hesitation, and a blockage as we seek to move past a moment or situation in our lives. But we don't have to remain confused and stagnant. When we commit our thoughts and ways unto God, He directs our paths. His thoughts are not ours (Is. 55:8). He is past, present, and future (Rev.1:8). He is the beginning and the end (Rev.1:8). So, when teaching becomes confusing, cumbersome, or simply overwhelming, steal away, submit your concerns to Him, and remind yourself of these truths.

Weekly Application:

As you teach this week, lean not on your own understanding, but seek direction from God who can carve a straight path for you. You find this direction in the Word of God.

Reread the scriptures below.
    Is. 55:8, THE MESSAGE
    Rev.1:8, THE MESSAGE
    Prov. 3:5-7, THE MESSAGE

Write the principle (s) from the scriptures you find will be most useful to you as you teach.

Reflection/Notes:

WEEK 32

It is Well

1. **Read the Scriptures.**
   Rom. 4:17, THE MESSAGE
   2 Kgs. 4:26, THE MESSAGE
2. **Read this week's teaching on it is well.**

It is Well. If we understood the power of our words, we'd be careful as
to what we speak. Too often, we have a tendency to speak of the negative; to speak of what is wrong. Too little pay; too many classes; too many
students; not enough resources for student support; not enough Human
Resources; classrooms are too small; too much traffic; and this list can
certainly continue. While many of these and your concerns may be valid,
as spirit-filled educators, we have a unique position to bring about change
in one or more of these areas. But first, we have to know in our hearts,
regardless of the present condition, that it is well.

In 2 Kgs. 4:26, the Shunnamite woman was facing total devastation.
The son that was promised to her, that she did not ask for, had died. It was
her only son. Yet, when the servant asked if everything was all right, she
replied, yes to him even though she knew her son had died.

The first lesson here is that she did not speak of the current negative
circumstance although it appeared to be permanent. As an educator, you

will be tempted to engage in conversations discussing or even complaining about certain issues. Don't. Continue to believe and speak "all is well."

In vv.27-28, while confessing all is well, she takes her concern to the one who could provide instruction to solve the problem. Herein lies the second lesson. Your concerns as an educator will be warranted. It is what you do with those concerns that matter. Pray about them first to God. Voice those concerns to Him. He will provide the resources needed; He will fill the deficit, or at least show you how to operate in the deficit. Finally, begin to thank Him for the provision and speak it into existence (Rom. 4:17). Use your voice to change circumstances; not to complain or gossip about them.

Weekly Application:

As you teach, use the power of your words to speak goodwill and tidings over your day, yourself, and those important to you. Having prayed, confess and believe *it is well.*

Reread the scriptures below.
Rom. 4:17, THE MESSAGE
2 Kgs. 4:26, THE MESSAGE

Write the principle (s) from the scriptures you find will be most useful to you as you teach.

Reflection/Notes:

WEEK 33

BELIEVE

1. **Read the Scriptures.**
     Heb. 11:6, THE MESSAGE
     Jhn. 4:49-50, THE MESSAGE
2. **Read this week's teaching on believe.**

Believe. Believe sounds easy, but actually *believing* is the challenging part for many. We are not alone. What concerns Jesus throughout scripture is disbelief. He encounters disbelief from his disciples and of course, the Pharisees. We have diligence in believing for what we consider to be minor things. We will believe him for healing, but not for a short check out line at the grocery store. We will believe him for a financial blessing, but not for better health. Truth is God wants us to believe Him for everything.

As an educator, we can be blindsided at any given moment in our classrooms. Educating a wide range of students from diverse backgrounds creates a recipe, daily, for conflicts varying in nature and intensity. When we enter our classrooms daily, we must truly believe we are not entering alone and that He has our best interest and protection at heart.

From active shooters to fights and verbal conflicts that can break out amongst the students, we must put our trust in God and believe that one day will be good because He is the creator of all of our days. Unbelief is what hinders our prayers in progress.

When we approach Him in prayer, we must believe that He is. We must believe He will reward us for our diligence. Believing is a challenge for many because we are being asked to believe in a being we cannot see. It is in this moment, you want to activate and rely on your faith.

Without faith, you cannot please the Lord; you must believe in your heart that you are praying to a living God (Heb. 11:6). In the end, take Him at His Word (Jhn. 4:49-50).

Weekly Application:

It is easy to say I believe, but harder for that belief to be in your heart. Your heart is where the truth is. Begin your day believing in your heart and confessing with your mouth that Jesus lives and belief in Him makes everyday possible. Don't doubt. Just believe.

Reread the scriptures below.
Heb. 11:6, THE MESSAGE
Jhn. 4:49-50, THE MESSAGE

Write the principle (s) from the scriptures you find will be most useful to you as you teach.

Reflection/Notes:

BASIC TRUTHS

1. **Read the Scriptures.**
   Heb. 6:1-11, THE MESSAGE
2. **Read this week's teaching on basic truths.**

B asic Truths. A basic truth is a fundamental element that serves as the foundation or building blocks for other truths. It is the foundation on which one believes career, health, and lifestyle are built. Putting into practice the basic truths supporting any of these areas in your life is an indication of growth and maturity.

For example, as an educator, you signed your teaching contract keenly aware of a few basic truths regarding the position. 1) Be in class on time. 2) Report absences to department head. 3) Teach all classes to which you are signed. 4) Pay periods are on the 15th and the last day of the month. Embracing these truths helps you to perform your job that much more efficiently.

You understand arriving to class on time can divert wayward behavior and reduce class conflict. You also know that there are dire complications for failing to show up for work to teach your classes. Because you know the dates of your pay, you will not expect your check on an off day.

Much in the same way, the writer of Hebrews 6 encourages us to embrace the basic truths of Christ and move on to His solid teachings. To embrace this truth means to become mature in them, believing and practicing so you are not to be taught them again and again. Just like maturity in the basic truths of teaching can enhance your teaching skills, maturing in the basic truth of Christ can enhance your prayer life tremendously by removing any barriers to your prayers to God for yourself and your students.

> Truth 1: show remorse for your sins and turn from them (v.1). When we believe we have disappointed God, it makes it difficult for us to approach Him in meditative prayer.

> Truth 2: Have faith, so you do not doubt (v. 11). Without faith, we can't please God for those who go To him, must believe that he is (v. 6).

> Truth 3: Be baptized (v.2). Being baptized cleanses you and shows your belief in the saving power of our Lord.

Stand firm on these truths to not have your prayers for yourself and students hindered in any way.

Weekly Application:

As you teach, show remorse for your sins and turn from them (v.1). When we believe we have disappointed God, it makes it difficult for us to approach Him in prayer.

Truth 2: Have faith, so you do not doubt (v. 11). Without faith, we can't please God for those who go to him, must believe that he is (v. 6).

Truth 3: Be baptized (v.2). Being baptized cleanses you and shows your belief in the saving power of our Lord.

Reread the scriptures below.
Heb. 6:1-11, THE MESSAGE

Write the principle (s) from the scriptures you find will be most useful to you as you teach.

Reflection/Notes:

LESSON PLAN

1. **Read the Scriptures.**
   Prov. 16:9, THE MESSAGE
2. **Read this week's teaching on the lesson plan.**

L esson Plan. Educators know lesson planning well. Objectives, Opening Set, Middle Set, Closing Set– all determined ahead of time and strategically purposed for the educational benefit of our students. Nevertheless, we do not want to rigidly adhere to our lesson plans leaving no room for creativity, flexibility, and the Holy Spirit. Prov. 16:9 reminds us that it is He who determines the order and outcome of the plans we make daily—even our lesson plans.

On the first day of my Oral Communication course, I decided to put a spin on the self introduction ice breakers where students would merely stand in front of the class and give a spiel about their hometown, name, major, and one interesting fact about themselves.

Instead, I had them to research the meaning of their names and its correlation to their personality traits. Then, impromptu style, I had students to introduce themselves sharing what they learned about their names. As students presented, I noticed a pattern and was pleasantly surprised by it. A few of the students' names had biblical meanings and they embraced the biblical meaning as being a reflection of their personality. As they shared, I heard references to Christlike, God's gifts, faith, and destiny. In just a few moments, the exercise evolved into a dialogue about our heavenly Father and His son Jesus Christ. I did not discourage this dialogue, but rather encouraged it by asking probing questions.

Unbeknownst to the students, they were dropping word seeds of encouragement, curiosity, and belief right there in the class. And it all stemmed from the meaning of their names. God's intervention is not limited to our personal plans; He can take over our classrooms too redirecting our lesson plans in a whole new way!

Weekly Application:

As you teach, yield your lesson plan to Him. Allow God to use it for His glory. Then, delight in the presence of the Lord and His work on the hearts and minds of your students.

Reread the scriptures below.
Prov. 16:9, THE MESSAGE

Write the principle (s) from the scriptures you find will be most useful to you as you teach.

Reflection/Notes:

SATISFACTION

1. **Read the Scriptures.**
   Ex. 33:14-15, THE MESSAGE
   Matt. 23:11, THE MESSAGE
2. **Read this week's teaching on satisfaction.**

Satisfaction. Food. Friends. Family. Careers. (I am certain you can add a few more categories to this list). Each has the potential to instill a form of satisfaction in our lives, but not the ultimate satisfaction. There is only one presence that brings us the ultimate satisfaction in our lives in the midst of all else.

Moses communicated with the Spirit of the Lord informing Him that if His presence did not accompany him, he did not want to go. Moses understood the sovereignty, power, omnipotence, and provision the Lord's Spirit brought with him. In Ex. 33, upon being instructed to journey into the land of milk and honey, the Lord informed Moses He would not accompany them [Moses and the Israelites] for he was displeased with their lack of obedience. Grieved, Moses communicated with the Lord at the Tent of Meeting informing Him that only His presence distinguishes them from others and indicates His pleasure in His people. Without His presence, he did not want to take this journey—vv. 14-15. Because Moses carried the Spirit of the Lord inside of Him byway of relationship, he was able to talk with the Lord, making a case for His presence to go along with them on their journey. He knew that without it, there would be no rest (v.14), protection (v. 2), or mercy and compassion (v. 19). There would be no ultimate satisfaction.

When a verbal dispute broke out between two of my female students in our Freshman Composition I course, I remained calm. When the verbal nearly escalated to physical, I still remained calm as I de-escalated the situation. I had to mind the safety of not only myself, but the other students in the course as well. I could not, however, have done either without the presence of the Lord there in that classroom with me that day.

As an educator, developing a relationship with the Lord maintains the health of your soul by reminding you of whose presence you need daily—especially in your classrooms. While the eyes of the Lord are in every place, His Spirit is not; we must welcome and invoke His Spirit where we desire Him to be—for educators, this means inviting Him into our classrooms to experience an ultimate satisfaction. Our human efforts and knowledge do not replace the presence of God. While we may find satisfaction in our teaching accolades, offices, or the faculty lounge, this satisfaction is only surface deep. It can be disturbed by the smallest of infractions. But when we know whose presence is with us, we can face the challenges of this week, and every week, boldly.

Weekly Application:

As you teach, remember to invoke the presence of the Lord to accompany you in your classrooms and anywhere else your feet may tread.

Reread the scriptures below.
> Ex. 33:14-15, THE MESSAGE
> Matt. 23:11, THE MESSAGE

Write the principle (s) from the scriptures you find will be most useful to you as you teach.

Reflection/Notes:

IN CLOSING, ENCOURAGE YOURSELF.

Encourage Yourself

When You Say or Think: I am tired.

Encourage Yourself:

"Are you tired? Worn out? Burned out on religion? Come to me. Get away with me and you'll recover your life. I'll show you how to and work with me—watch how I do it. Learn the unforced rhythms of grace. I won't lay anything heavy or ill-fitting on you. Keep company with me and you'll learn to live freely and lightly"

Matt. 11:28-30, THE MESSAGE

When You Say or Think: I am not good enough. I simply do not measure up.

Encourage Yourself:

"Oh yes, you shaped me first inside, then out; you formed me in my mother's womb.I thank you, High God—you're breathtaking!

Body and soul, I am marvelously made!

I worship in adoration—what a creation!

You know me inside and out, you know every bone in my body;

You know exactly how I was made, bit by bit,

how I was sculpted from nothing into something.

Like an open book, you watched me grow from conception to birth;

all the stages of my life were spread out before you,

The days of my life all prepared

before I'd even lived one day"

Pslm.139:14, THE MESSAGE

When You Say or Think: I am afraid.
Encourage Yourself:

God doesn't want us [me] to be shy with his gifts, but bold and loving and sensible.

2 Tim. 1:7, THE MESSAGE

When You Say or Think: I am not strong enough.
Encourage Yourself:

Whatever I have, wherever I am, I can make it through anything in the One who makes me who I am.

Phil. 4:13, THE MESSAGE

When You Say or Think: I don't think God hears me.
Encourage Yourself:

My purpose in writing is simply this: that you who believe in God's Son will know beyond the shadow of a doubt that you have eternal life, the reality and not the illusion. And how bold and free we then become in his presence, freely asking according to his will, sure that he's listening.

1 Jhn. 5:13-14, THE MESSAGE

When You Say or Think: I don't have enough.
Encourage Yourself:

You can be sure that God will take care of everything you need, his generosity exceeding even yours in the glory that pours from Jesus.

Phil. 4:19, THE MESSAGE

When You Say or Think: I am depressed.
Encourage Yourself:

All you saints! Sing
your hearts out to God!
Thank him to his face!
He gets angry once in a while, but across
a lifetime there is only love.

The nights of crying your eyes out
give way to days of laughter.

Pslm. 30:5, THE MESSAGE

When You Say or Think: I give up.
Encourage Yourself:

Why would you ever
complain, O Jacob,
or, whine, Israel, saying,
"God has lost track of me.
He doesn't care what happens to me"?
Don't you know anything? Haven't you been listening?
God doesn't come and go. God lasts.
He's Creator of all you can see or imagine.
He doesn't get tired out, doesn't pause to catch his breath.
And he knows everything, inside and out.
He energizes those who get tired,
gives fresh strength to dropouts.
For even young people tire and drop out,
young folk in their prime stumble and fall.
But those who wait upon God get fresh strength.
They spread their wings and soar like eagles,
They run and don't get tired,
they walk and don't lag behind.

As an educator, be encouraged and encourage yourself. The possibilities are endless for you and you have the potential for your influence to be vast. We need divine power to teach, which can only come from a divine source; we need a servant's heart to put others' needs before our own, and to perform as effectively as possible daily, we need to know the true source of our help and understand that it is not merely our ability. Continue to encourage your soul often through meditative prayers to Jesus Christ, the son of the living God, and be renewed daily.

I will instruct you and teach you in the way you should go; I will counsel you with my loving eye on you.
PSALM 32:8

Acknowledgements

To my students, colleagues, and administrators—thank you for allowing me to teach, serve, and lead in one or more areas of your lives.

To my friends, family, pastoral leaders, and Kevin—thank you for your unwavering support. May God continue to bless each of you.

About the Author

Stacey Reed is a Christian educator and professor. She earned her Bachelor of Arts in English degree from Benedict College and Master of Arts in English degree from Stephen F. Austin State University. She has completed extensive study in the Teaching of English at Coastal Carolina University, Organizational Leadership at Charleston Southern University, and Higher Education Administration at Concordia University-Portland.

She has received various awards for her teaching, leadership, and dedication to education including the Educator's Appreciation Award from Gospel Missionary Baptist Church in Georgetown, SC and the Outstanding Leadership Award for service performed as Vice President and President of the National Association of African American Honors Programs for Historically Black Colleges and Universities.

Stacey is a member of the Christian Educators Association International (CEAI). She continues to teach, lead, and serve while sharing the good news.

SHARE ENCOURAGEMENT!
Social Media/Facebook:
@MorningMusingsEncouragement

SIGN UP FOR TEACHING DEVOTIONALS!
www.staceydreed.com

JOIN OUR BOOK CLUB!
www.staceydreed.com